POOR

TRADERS

AND

INVESTORS

DEDICATION

I dedicate my book to God almighty who has been my source of knowledge, wisdom and strength.

ACKNOWLEDGEMENTS

My profound gratitude and appreciation goes to God Almighty who is my source of strength. May I use this medium to show gratitude to My parent Mr and Mrs Gyana, my brothers and sisters Mrs Mery Gata, Joseph Gyana and also my friends Ocholi Augustine Egahi for their advice and encouragement.

TABLE OF CONTENTS

★ TRADERS

★ FUNDRAISE

★ RESPONSIBILITY FOR TRADERS

★ INVESTORS

★ WHAT TO AVOIDING DOING

★ CONCLUSION

INTRODUCTION

If you have studied and created a good market strategy that you have backtested, better you should start with the money that you have. When you start with little money, you should proof that you use very small lot sizes. Doing this will proof that you decrease the amount of danger that you take for your business. Of course, the amount of profit that you can make with these lot sizes is not very much, but it will support your business.

CHAPTER ONE

TRADERS

You're a trader, and you just don't seem to be making any headway. You keep losing money, and you're starting to feel like you're just not cut out for this. You've tried every strategy out there, but nothing seems to be working. Some people don't know that to start trading they're things or steps you need to take before seeing the success of your market why some people don't want to follow the main steps before they start marketing and they're need to study the business and the area where they want to start the business. Not all traders know somethings like this and as a trader before buying a goods you have to first look at the quality of products that you want to order from company before you start marketing because in most companies each product has it own productivity quality and price. The most common challenge We hear from traders is that they don't have enough money to trade.

This is a common stumper that many traders combat at the beginning of their careers and some may collect loan but still yet the business will still collapse as a trader not all business, you start and apply for a loan. Before a trader apply for a loan he/she needs to check how the business is growing and what will be his/her profit end of every month and if trader find out that the profits of the business will be low the trader need to avoid applying for loan. Not all business require or need loan before the business will be successful what matters is how the trader plans that matters. Knowledge is the most important assets that you can have as a trader. You can have all the money but without knowledge, you will loose all your capital. We have seen people start their trading with more than $5,000 only to lose it within a short period of time.

Even before thinking about the money that trader have, should focus on gaining the knowledge and skillfulness to become a better trader. This knowledge should come from others traders that has been into the system for number of years because these type of traders has experience many problems when it comes to business and if you are still new as a market trader, you should start small. Good thing is that you can start purchase of goods with the little amount of money. There are still companies that accept traders to purchase little amount of goods but base on the amount of money that a trader have.

CHAPTER TWO

FUNDRAISE

After your business is sugary for a lank time, you should now start to fundraise to get more money. By funding more capital, you will be able to get more money that you can buy more goods to expend your business. Moreover, no one will give you money to expend your business if you don't have quality in the market.

For example, if you started a business with just $800 and reached $1800 profit within a period of more than one year. With such a track record, you can approach apply for a loan from your friends. You should ask your friends or family to help you with fund and then moving to other people who might be interested in to loan you some funds. I advise that you return money to your friends that lend you funds and use your own money only when you have made good money. Regressive money will remove the obligate that you have when trading.

Instead, you can return the funds that your friends gave you, then you can continue business with the profits that you have made. This is also a way of removing higher risks and obligate of losing money.

CHAPTER THREE

RESPONSIBILITY FOR TRADERS

As you will realize, starting a business with your own money is more fulfilling than applying for a loan when you are still new in marketing. This is because when buying goods for yourself, you have total control. You can decide not to buy any goods for a week and no one will question you.

However, when buy goods with others people money that when you will try to meet up and to make huge profit before the end of the period you agreed to return the money that you borrowed , although it will make you more money, has its challenges. For instance, you must always modify them on what is going on in the market. You must also verify that you don't lose money for your business. This is the hard part.

To avoid the risk of legal issue in case the money is lost, you should ensure that you others ways to return the money that you agreed to take any losses. we have various ways to take responsibility for traders and this includes:

I. Manage Your Risks

II. Don't Leverage Too Much

III. Position Your Business

IV. A Good Strategy

I. MANAGE YOUR RISKS

A common rational motive why people don't manage to grow their business is known as risk management. Having a good risk management plan will go a long way in helping you become a successful trader for long period of time. Fortunately, there are respective risk management strategies you can use.

II. DON'T LEVERAGE TOO MUCH

First, you should use a relatively small supply. Doing this will help to decrease the risks involved in running a relatively oversupplied business. You can start small and then increase the Supply as you gain more experience.

III. POSITION YOUR BUSINESS

Second, always position your business well. Since you are starting small, buying large products of goods can have a meaningful impact on your trades if things go wrong. Therefore, hold your business plan well and then increase your strategy as your investment grow.

IV. A GOOD STRATEGY

Third, you should have a well-tested business strategy. Just take your time to business and test your strategy.

Other risk management strategies you should stop buying a large quantities of goods at first time that you start bausiness.

CHAPTER FOUR

INVESTORS

There are many investors who struggle to make a profit. But the good news is that there are things you can do to turn it around. Every business trader or investor has a mission and they usually know why they are in business. Under Force wants to do great sports workwear, Steve Jobs believed in Apple and a design-driven tech company, the IKEA founder loved building things, Mark Zuckerberg wanted to create a social media network for people from different places to meet each other and also to promote business on his social media network. Thomas Edison was a passionate inventor, Elon Musk wants to take the world to the next level that will benefit humanity.

Reasons why investors fail, and we'll give you some guidance on how to overcome challenges these includes:

I. Why Do People Traders And Investors Struggle?

II. Successful And Unsuccessful Traders And Investors

III. How To Turn It Around And Become Successful

IV. The Most Important Things To Focus On

I. WHY DO PEOPLE TRADERS AND INVESTORS STRUGGLE?

You might be wondering why some traders and investors are poor. The answer is simple: they struggle because they don't have a god strategy.

A lot of people think that trading and investing is all about making quick profits. But if you're not careful, you can easily lose money in a short period of time. That's why it's important to have a good idea and stay disciplined in business. If you're not following a plan, then you're basically flying by the place of your pants, and that's a direction for disaster. So ask yourself this question: are you trading or investing for the short term or the long term? Because if it's the former, then you're going to have a hard time succeeding in the markets.

II. SUCCESSFUL AND UNSUCCESSFUL TRADERS AND INVESTORS

Before we get into how to turn things around, let's take a quick look at the difference between successful and unsuccessful traders and investors.

Successful traders and investors have a plan. They know their goals, they know their limits, and they stick to their plan. They're also patient—they're not looking to make a quick buck. They're in it for a long period of time.

Unsuccessful traders and investors, on the other hand, tend to be impulsive. They make decisions based on feeling, rather than sense. And they're not willing to put in the hard work required to succeed.

If you want to be a successful trader or investor, you need to have a plan and you need to be patient. You need to be able to stay calm under pressure and make smart decisions based on sense, not feeling. It's not going to be easy, but it's worth it in the end.

Unsuccessful traders and investors always think of how they will make quick profits and they don't think of how to grow their business. If you want to grow your business you need to take care of your business or investment. Some traders end up spending their capital with other things that will not multiply profit and as a trader or investor you need to minimize spend money unnecessary things.

III. HOW TO TURN IT AROUND AND BECOME SUCCESSFUL

So you want to be a successful trader or investor? It's not going to be easy for you, but it is possible only if you can obey this words of knowledge. Here are a few tips to help you turn it around and become successful:

1. Get organized. This means having a plan and always sticking to it. Always think we'll before you purchase any products and check how much is your profit end of every goods you sales.

2. Learn as much as you can. Knowledge is power, and the more you know about the markets, the better equipped you'll be to make smart decisions.

3. Stay disciplined. This is key—you need to have the discipline to stay in the game even when things aren't going your way.

4. Take your losses seriously. Don't let your ego get in the way—if you're wrong, admit it and move on.

5. Have patience. Rome wasn't built in a day, and success as a trader or investor doesn't happen overnight. Be patient and stay the course, and you'll see results eventually.

6. Keep records of every products that you sales this will help you to know the extectly products that gives you profit every end of the month.

IV. THE MOST IMPORTANT THINGS TO FOCUS ON

You're probably wondering what the most important things are to focus on if you want to become a successful trader or investor. Well, here are tips that will set you in the right direction.

First, develop a plan and stick to it. Don't try to reinvent the wheel every time you step into the market. Have a good strategy and make sure you understand all the risks before you put your money on the line.

Second, keep a cool head and don't let your emotions get the best of you. This is easier said than done, but if you can stay focused and objective, you'll be more likely to make rational decisions that could end up saving you a lot of money. Product sometimes matter as a trader try to focus on a particular products or goods that will fetch you more profit because not all traders know the particular products that is selling best. While some just decided to purchase anyhow goods and this will affect your business.

Always do your research. Know who you're dealing with, know what the market is doing, know your own limitations. Education is key in this game, so never stop learning and expanding your knowledge base. As an investor you always need to travel round it expend your knowledge about new business to invest your money but always make a signed agreement with you and the company that you want to invest your money.

CHAPTER FIVE

WHAT TO AVOIDING DOING

When it comes to trading and investing, you need to be aware of the common mistakes that people make. And if you want to be a successful trader or investor, you need to avoid these mistakes at all cost.

One of the biggest mistakes that people are making in business is that they want to make over profit. They think that they need to follow every market trend and invest in every hot stock. But this is a recipe for disaster.

Another mistake is not paying attention to the fundamentals. You need to have a solid understanding of the company's financials before you invest in its stock.

As a tradeer you need to study the type of business you want to start because most trader don't even take steps to know what type of business will be suitable for them and that will much profits them.

As an investor not anyhow company you need to invest your money into because not all companies can meet up this can cause lose of money.

Lastly, don't trade or invest based on your emotions. Trading and investing should be a rational process, not a guessing game.

They're things investors and traders need to keep away from and research these includes :

  I. Common Mistakes Poor Traders And Investors Make

  II. Ways To Avoid Failure In Your Business

  III. About Your Business

I. COMMON MISTAKES POOR TRADERS AND INVESTORS MAKE

You might be wondering why some traders and investors seem to struggle while others seem to make a treasure. The reason is that most people make the same mistakes over and over again. Here are some of the most common mistakes that poor traders and investors make:

1. They don't take the time to learn about the markets.

2. They don't have a trading or investment plan.

3. They trade or invest based on emotions, rather than sense.

4. They let fear and greed dictate their trading and investment decisions.

5. They don't have enough capital to trade or invest with.

6. They trade or invest based on guidance or rumors they've heard.

7. They don't take losses seriously and keep holding on to losing trades too long.

II. WAYS TO AVOID FAILURE IN YOUR BUSINESS

A person who wants to avoid business failure must work hard.

He must think and find the work to do

He must not sit down and laugh when others go out for business.

He must think and plan for tomorrow.

He must avoid spending his money carelessly.

He must be truthful and humble.

He must not find troubles.

He must bear insults.

He must be wise and careful.

He must be neat and clever.

He must avoid enemies and bad companies.

He must think well before he decides.

He must know his monthly income and expenses.

He must be serious over his work.

He must have respect.

He must be obedient.

He must not talk against others, so that they may not talk against him.

III. ABOUT YOUR BUSINESS

He who seeks for money and wants to get it must not say that the sun is too much, he must work under it.

He must be honest and truthful always.

He must not say that the hot weather is coming, he must work under it.

He must sing his favourite song and work.

He must not fear work

He must work hard.

He must be obedient.

He must be humble.

He must be punctual to his work.

He must endure insult and abuse.

He must not cause trouble of any kind.

He must not play with his business.

He must improve his handwork in order to attract more customers than others trades.

He must not charge too much.

He must not play with his business, otherwise his business may failed.

CONCLUSION

It can be tough to be a poor trader or investor. You may feel like you're always on the losing end of things, and that you can't seem to catch a break. But don't worry, you're not alone. A lot of traders and investors find themselves in this position, and there are ways to turn it all around.

In this post, we'll talk about why poor traders and investors struggle in the first place, and what you can do to turn it all around. So keep reading to learn more!

ABOUT THE AUTHOR

Joseph Monday Gyana is a Nigerian writer born on 25th May 1993 from Nasarawa State located in the northcentral part of Nigeria. He is the last in his family he had his elementary school in L. E. A primary school angwandodo gwagwalada Abuja (2000-2007). He then got admitted in to ST. Pual college high school where he bagged his west Africa examination council certificate in 2013. During this period, Joseph Monday Gyana loves computer programming and was known to be the best in his pairs but due to the fact that his Dad wanted him to study in the university he had to quit football. His very good on HML, CSS, JAVASCRIPT, JAVA, JSON and XML programming languages and his also good on crypto currency and Blockchain technology.

www.ingramcontent.com/pod-product-compliance
Lightning Source LLC
Chambersburg PA
CBHW080440220526
45465CB00009B/3366